Community Helpers

Preschool/Kindergarten

Table of Contents

Thematic Units

More Activities and Ideas

Reproducible Activities

Save time and energy planning thematic units with this comprehensive resource. We've searched the 1990–1998 issues of **The MAILBOX**® and *Teacher's Helper*® magazines to find the best ideas for you to use when teaching a thematic unit about community helpers. Included in this book are favorite units from the magazines, single ideas to extend a unit, and a variety of reproducible activities. Use these activities to develop your own complete unit or simply to enhance your current lesson plans. You're sure to find everything you need for strengthening student learning.

Project Managers: Sherri Lynn Kuntz, Scott Lyons
Copy Editors: Sylvan Allen, Gina Farago, Karen Brewer Grossman, Karen L. Huffman, Amy Kirtley-Hill, Debbie Shoffner
Cover Artists: Nick Greenwood, Kimberly Richard
Artist: Jennifer L. Tipton
Typesetters: Lynette Dickerson, Mark Rainey

President, The Mailbox Book Company™: Joseph C. Bucci
Director of Book Planning and Development: Chris Poindexter
Book Development Managers: Stephen Levy, Elizabeth H. Lindsay, Thad McLaurin, Susan Walker
Curriculum Director: Karen P. Shelton
Traffic Manager: Lisa K. Pitts
Librarian: Dorothy C. McKinney
Editorial and Freelance Management: Karen A. Brudnak
Editorial Training: Irving P. Crump
Editorial Assistants: Terrie Head, Hope Rodgers, Jan E. Witcher

www.themailbox.com

Manufactured in the United States
10 9 8 7 6 5 4 3

Thematic Units...

U.S. MAIL

WHEN I GROW UP...

by Lucia Kemp Henry

Take a fresh approach to career studies with these activities. A reproducible gameboard, student-made booklet, and worksheets are designed to minimize your preparation time.

School Careers

Although they observe school personnel daily, students are frequently unaware of their job titles or exactly what they do. Take photographs of the school staff including the nurse, cook, janitor, secretary, bus driver, teacher's aide, and principal. Post the photographs on a bulletin board. Under each photo, post a brief job description. (For example: I am the school nurse. I take care of sick children.) Then ask school personnel to speak to your students about their jobs and give tours of their workstations.

"I Can Work Outdoors" Booklet

Creating this booklet gives youngsters an opportunity to picture themselves in several outdoor-oriented careers. Prepare for the activity by duplicating pages 7–12 on white construction paper for each student. On pages 7–11, cut on the dotted lines with an X-acto knife. Staple each set of booklet pages between colorful covers. To the inside back cover of each booklet, attach a student's picture so that his face shows through the opening in each page. (If pictures are not available, each student may draw his face on the inside back cover of the booklet.)

Discuss each occupation and its environment before having students color the figure and background. Have students color and attach the corresponding pieces from page 12 to complete each scene. (Or provide a variety of magazine cutouts for students to use.)

Let's Go! Lotto

Focus on transportation-related careers with this lotto game. On tagboard, duplicate the lotto pieces and gameboard on page 6. Have each student cut out the patterns and match the vehicle cards to the occupations represented on the gameboard. Then have students discuss other careers that are dependent on vehicles.

Career Chorus

To introduce service-oriented careers, have a sing-along! Sing these verses to the tune of "Farmer in the Dell," and then have students create more verses.

Verse 1:
A farmer works his fields.
A farmer works his fields.
Hi, Ho, the derry-o,
A farmer works his fields.

Chorus:
There are so many jobs
That you might want to do.
Take time and you will find a job
That's just right for you.

Verse 2:
A dentist cleans our teeth.
Repeat Chorus
Verse 3:
A teacher works at school.
Repeat Chorus
Verse 4:
A barber cuts our hair.
Repeat Chorus
Verse 5:
A waiter serves us food.
Repeat Chorus

I am a ranger. I work in a park.

Occupation Scrapbook

Give children a chance to learn about careers and to share their knowledge with others. Have students clip magazine pictures of people at work. Discuss the clippings and determine the occupations associated with them. Compile the pictures in a class scrapbook and have students dictate sentences about each occupation. Store the scrapbook in your reading area and invite students to look at it during spare time.

This man is a nurse. He takes care of sick people. Toby's mom is a nurse, too!

"When I Grow Up..." Bulletin Board

Have students illustrate the jobs they find most appealing. (Discuss a wide range of career options.) Then ask students to draw large pictures of themselves in the careers of their choice. (Or have students select and glue magazine pictures to construction paper.) Then write the sentence at the bottom of each child's picture as he completes this statement: "I want to be a..." Post these portraits on a bulletin board for all to see!

Career Kits

Gather props to encourage role play of various careers. From postal workers, for example, you might borrow an old mailbag, a postman's hat and jacket, a rubber stamp, and a zip-code book. Paint a sturdy, produce box red, white, and blue. Then fill it with junk mail, a cardboard sectional divider (for sorting of mail), and the other props. Make several different career kits. Introduce them to the dramatic play area one at a time.

Check Your Resources

Use the career-education resources that are available to you.

- Take field trips that will give students insights into career opportunities. Be sure to include visits to a local fire station, police department, hospital, grocery store, dentist's office, beauty salon, park, library, bank, orchard, mall, or farm.
- Show films about careers. Children especially love to see films that tell how things are made and about the people who make them.
- Invite guest speakers into your classroom. People with interesting hobbies or talents make great teachers—especially if they demonstrate their skills.
- Check out a variety of library books about careers. Begin with *What People Do* from the Let's Discover series, Raintree Publishers, Inc.
- Begin discussions with study prints. Your school library or resource center may have a collection of study prints designed to stimulate discussions on careers.

Patterns

Use with "Let's Go! Lotto" on page 4.

Gameboard

Let's Go! Lotto

I am a farmer. I work on a farm.

Note to the teacher: Use with " 'I Can Work Outdoors' Booklet" on page 4.

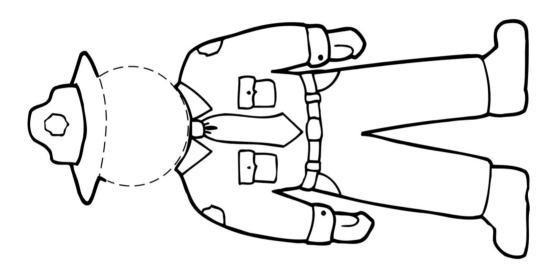

I am a ranger. I work in a park.

©The Education Center, Inc. • *Community Helpers* • Preschool/Kindergarten • TEC3234

Note to the teacher: Use with " 'I Can Work Outdoors' Booklet" on page 4.

I am a scuba diver. I work underwater.

3

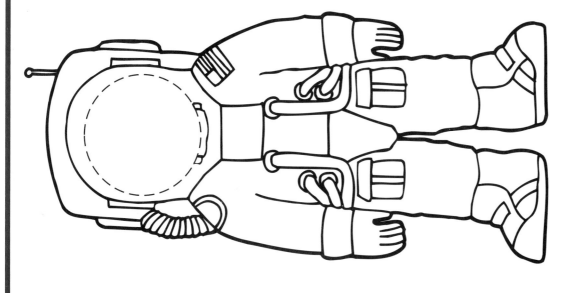

I am an astronaut. I work in space.

©The Education Center, Inc. • *Community Helpers* • Preschool/Kindergarten • TEC3234

Note to the teacher: Use with " 'I Can Work Outdoors' Booklet" on page 4.

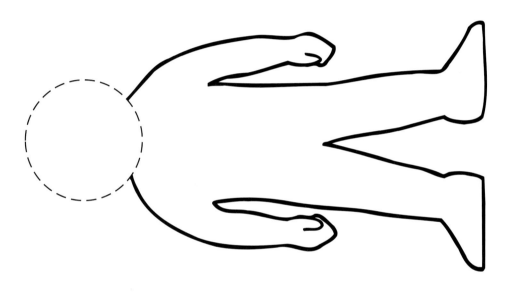

This is me. I am working outdoors.

Note to the teacher: Use with " 'I Can Work Outdoors' Booklet" on page 4.

Patterns

Use with "'I Can Work Outdoors' Booklet" on page 4.

Making

Do you like to make pretty pictures?

You can be an illustrator, a painter, or a photographer.

Cut and paste to make a picture.

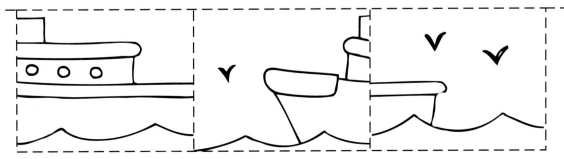

13

Helping

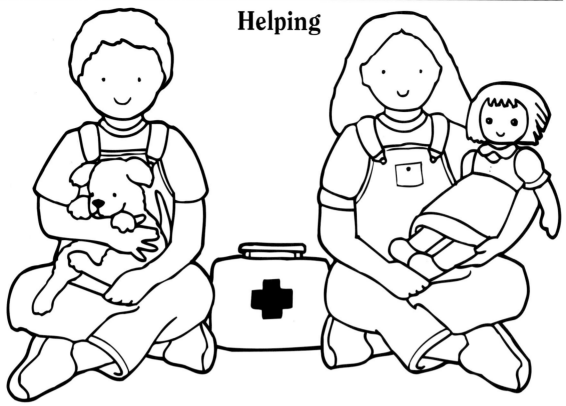

Do you like to care for dolls and pets?

You can be a doctor, a nurse, or a veterinarian.

Color the picture.

Trace.

Some people like to

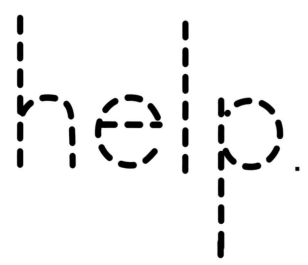

Imagining

Do you like to
make up stories?

You can be a writer,
a film director, or
an actor.

Color the things writers use.

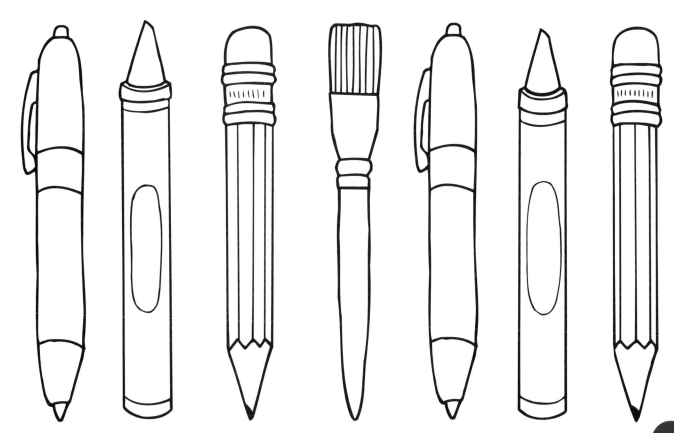

Driving

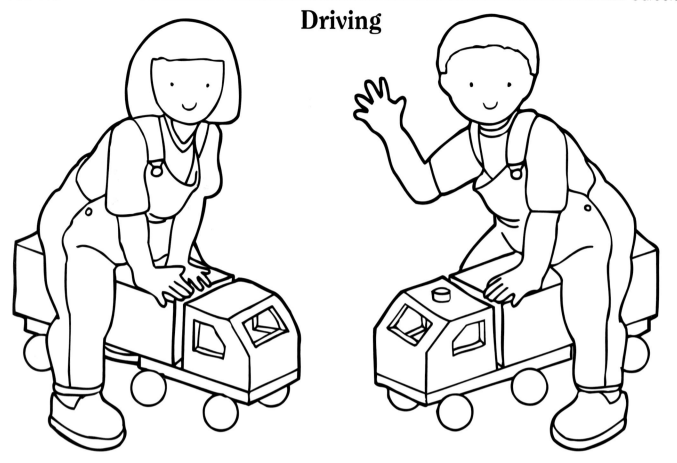

Do you like to play with trucks?

You can be a truck driver, a mechanic, or a factory worker.

Follow the dots.

Color.

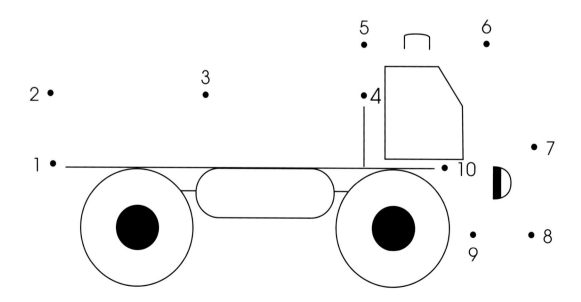

Building

Do you like to build
with blocks?

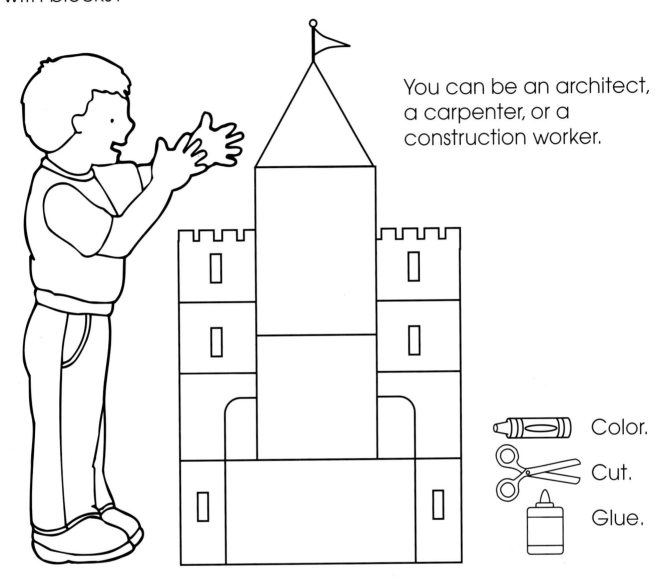

You can be an architect,
a carpenter, or a
construction worker.

Color.

Cut.

Glue.

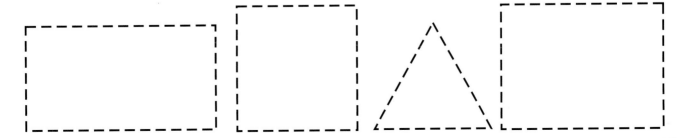

Heigh-Ho, Heigh-Ho, It's Off to Work We Go!

Here's a collection of work-related books and activities designed to give your youngsters on-the-job training about their future career options. These hardworking ideas offer big payoffs when it comes to increasing your students' career savvy as well as their curricular skills. And the fringe benefits are priceless—student pride in the work they do!

by Mackie Rhodes

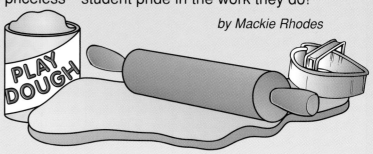

Daddies at Work
Mommies at Work
By Eve Merriam
Illustrated by Eugenie Fernandes
Published by Aladdin Paperbacks, 1989

Daddies and mommies everywhere perform many labors of love for their children. But what else do daddies and mommies do? With simple, sensitive text and gentle illustrations, these books introduce youngsters to the world of work outside the home. These particular selections might also spark children's curiosity about their own parents' jobs.

After reading and discussing these books, create a class collage to help children focus their attention on what parents or other adults might do at their jobs. To begin, provide a supply of blank paper and old magazines. Ask each child to cut out a picture of a person at work or of job-related tools. Then have her write (or dictate) about her picture. Next, help her glue the writing and the picture on a length of butcher paper titled "Everybody's Working." When each child has contributed to the collage, display it along a classroom wall and use it to reference various jobs during your career studies and to prompt dramatic play ideas. Look—everybody's working!

She grows flowers.

I Am Me!
By Alexa Brandenberg
Published by Red Wagon Books, 1996

What will you do when you grow up? In this book, nine young children aspire to careers that involve doing what they already like to do as children. Simple text and multicultural illustrations inspire readers to dream of all the possibilities!

This book—along with natural curiosity—makes a perfect springboard for career explorations! To begin, add simple props and costumes to your existing centers to transform them into different job locations. For example, make your housekeeping area a restaurant by adding menus, notepads, and pencils. Turn your block area into a fire station by providing fire helmets, hoses (made from wrapping paper tubes with silver-tinsel water), and red and orange tissue paper flames taped to block buildings. Transform your writing area into a post office by supplying a cardboard mailbox, stamps, envelopes, paper, and mailbags. Convert your art area into a bakery by adding play dough, cookie cutters, rolling pins, trays, chef hats, and aprons. Encourage children to visit these centers and pretend to be the workers and the customers. During group times, invite children to share what types of playing or jobs they like. Lots of food for thought here!

Mom Goes to Work

By Libby Gleeson
Illustrated by Penny Azar
Published by Scholastic Inc., 1992

A group of children stay busy at school while their moms work at their respective jobs. Parallel pictorials depict the simultaneous activities of children and their working parents—and cleverly convey the message that children have jobs, too!

After sharing this book, use the following home-school connection activity to expand students' career awareness and their understanding of the work done by their parents and other adults in their lives.

For each child, you'll need
1 copy of the poem on page 21
1 sheet of construction paper
2 half-sheets of construction paper
2 lengths of thick yarn
art supplies for decorating
access to a stapler
glue

Instruct each child to make a job bag by folding the whole sheet of construction paper in half. Have each child glue the poem to one side of her bag. Then help her staple along the sides of the bag, leaving the top open. Next, have each child glue yarn handles on the bag and decorate it as she likes.

When the job bags are finished, have each child make two job cards by folding her half-sheets of construction paper. Have her store one of the folded job cards in her bag and then reopen the remaining one. On the open card, invite her to illustrate and write about (dictate) a job that she is responsible for at home or at school. Then instruct the child to refold the job card and slide it into her job bag. Invite each child to take her bag home and share her job card with a family member or friend. Encourage each child to ask her partner at home to use the blank job card to illustrate and write about his own job. As the job bags come back to school, invite each child to share both job cards with the group; then mount her bag and cards on a board titled "Jobs in the Bag!"

Jobs People Do

By Christopher Maynard
Published by Dorling Kindersley Publishing, Inc.; 1997

This treasury of careers provides a first-person description of each featured occupation along with a photo of a child modeling related career gear. Additional photos and smaller text offer more details if interest dictates. It's a career wish book that will send imaginations soaring!

Integrate career awareness, listening skills, and lots of creativity with this idea. After sharing the book, ask each child to think of an occupation that he finds interesting. Encourage him to bring items from home and to use classroom art supplies to make related gear. Photograph each child in his outfit; then mount each photo on tagboard. Next, divide the photos into groups of five and add a cassette tape to each set. Color-code each piece of each different set. Then have each child record a first-person description of his career choice on the appropriate tape, leaving a pause between each narration. Label the back of each photo according to the order in which it is recorded on the tape. Store each photo-tape set in a separate zippered plastic bag; then place all the sets in your listening center. To do this activity, have a child choose a set, listen to the tape, and then sequence the pictures to correspond to the recorded descriptions. And what, may I ask, do *you* do?

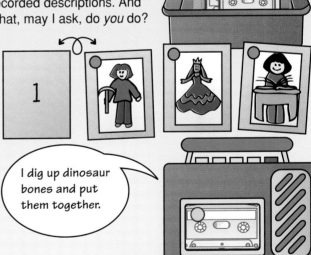

I dig up dinosaur bones and put them together.

That's easy!	That's hard!
5	15

What You Do Is Easy, What I Do Is Hard
By Jake Wold & Illustrated by Anna Dewdney
Published by Greenwillow Books, 1996

A boastful squirrel claims that he accomplishes the hardest jobs of all...until he is challenged to trade places with a bee, a robin, a spider, and an ant! Sweetly comical illustrations will have youngsters giggling as they ponder the strengths and weaknesses of each character—and themselves!

After sharing this story, guide children to summarize that each person has different skills and abilities that might make her better suited to some jobs than to others. Then invite youngsters to explore the variety of strengths and weaknesses among themselves—and sneak in a little math practice, too! To prepare, draw a two-column graph on the board. Label one column "That's Easy!" and the other "That's Hard!" Call out a skill such as, "Snap your fingers" or, "Hop on one foot"; then invite youngsters to try it. (It's helpful and fun to include a skill or two that you, the teacher, have difficulty doing—perhaps whistling or push-ups?) After each activity, have each child (and you!) attach a sticky note in the column that corresponds to her reaction to the given skill. Afterward, determine how many children thought that skill was easy and how many thought it was hard. Repeat the process as desired; then encourage children to talk about the variety of their strengths and weaknesses.

Guess Who?
By Margaret Miller
Published by Greenwillow Books, 1994

Who enjoys a guessing game that sparks interactive enthusiasm about jobs? Every reader of this Margaret Miller creation, of course! It's irresistible!

After sharing this story, your youngsters will be ready for this game version of *Guess Who?* In advance, photocopy, color, and laminate the job cards on pages 22–24; then cut them apart. Choose a small group of students and give each of those students a different job card. Have the group stand in front of the class. In turn, encourage each child to prompt the rest of the class to guess who (what occupation) is pictured on his card. Instruct those children to use clues that begin with *who,* such as "Who gives a dog a checkup?" or "Who serves food at a restaurant?" After all the workers have been guessed, give a different group of children new job cards; then play another round. Guess who is having lots of learning fun?

"Who serves food at a restaurant?"

"Who gives a dog a checkup?"

Grandmother's Alphabet
By Eve Shaw
Published by Pfeifer-Hamilton Publishers, 1997

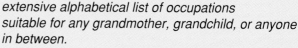

Grandma can be anything—and so can I! Beautiful illustrations and sensitive text offer an extensive alphabetical list of occupations suitable for any grandmother, grandchild, or anyone in between.

Reinforce career awareness and beginning sounds with this job-related idea. After sharing the book, invite each child to draw a picture of himself doing a job. When each child shares his illustration, guide the class to determine the beginning sound of the job represented. Then invite the artist to use a marker to label his illustration with that letter. Use a metal ring to bind all the pictures together in alphabetical order behind a title page. Throughout your career studies, encourage each child to add illustrations to the class-made book as he discovers additional jobs that interest him. In between *A* and *Z*, there's a very special job for me!

More Work-Related Literature

I Love You, Mom
By Iris Hiskey Arno
Illustrated by Joan Holub
Published by WhistleStop®, 1997

In this special tribute, children boast about their talented and hardworking moms!

Mr. Griggs' Work
By Cynthia Rylant
Illustrated by Julie Downing
Published by Orchard Books, 1989

Old Mr. Griggs loves his job at the post office! This man's steadfast devotion makes for a refreshing tale and a lesson in taking satisfaction and pride in our own work.

My Great-Aunt Arizona
By Gloria Houston
Illustrated by Susan Condie Lamb
Published by HarperCollins Publishers, 1992

Arizona loved to read and dream about the faraway places that she would one day visit—but life's circumstances kept her close to home. Eventually Arizona became the teacher at her old one-room school—and she taught there for 57 years! Those touched by her life carry her in their minds wherever they go.

Pig Pig Gets a Job
By David McPhail
Published by Dutton Children's Books, 1990

When Pig Pig announces that he wants to buy something, his mother surprises him by suggesting that he get a job. Together the two come up with an imaginative, practical way to help Pig Pig earn money and to take pride in his job.

During a class discussion about occupations, I asked one little girl what her daddy did for a living. She proudly replied, "My daddy is a souvenir!" Rather puzzled, I checked her file and discovered that her father was a *civil engineer!*

Leslie O'Donnell—Gr. K, Sedalia Park School
Marietta, Georgia

A Sign
By George Ella Lyon
Illustrated by Chris K. Soentpiet
Published by Orchard Books, 1998

A young girl's fascination with the jobs of a neon sign maker, a tightrope walker, and an astronaut inspire dreams about her own future. As an adult, she explores how her dreams shaped her career as a writer and the author of this book.

Work
By Ann Morris
Published by Lothrop, Lee & Shepard Books; 1998

Ann Morris' camera takes readers on a photographic journey around the world to observe all kinds of people doing all kinds of work. Vivid pictures and an informational index ignite interest in a variety of world cultures.

Worksong
By Gary Paulsen
Illustrated by Ruth Wright Paulsen
Published by Harcourt Brace & Company, 1997

With lyrical text and rich paintings, this song of praise celebrates the everyday jobs of people all over the world.

Order books on-line.
www.themailbox.com

Job Poem
Use with *Mom Goes to Work* on page 19.

Jobs
Mommies and daddies
And grandparents, too,
Are people with jobs—
With jobs that they do.

Aunts and uncles
And neighbors, it's true,
Are people with jobs—
With jobs that they do.

Boys and girls
Have jobs that they do.
I have a job—
How about YOU?

21

Job Cards

Use with *Guess Who?* on page 20.

doctor

referee

auto mechanic

scientist

author

police officer

Job Cards

Use with *Guess Who?* on page 20.

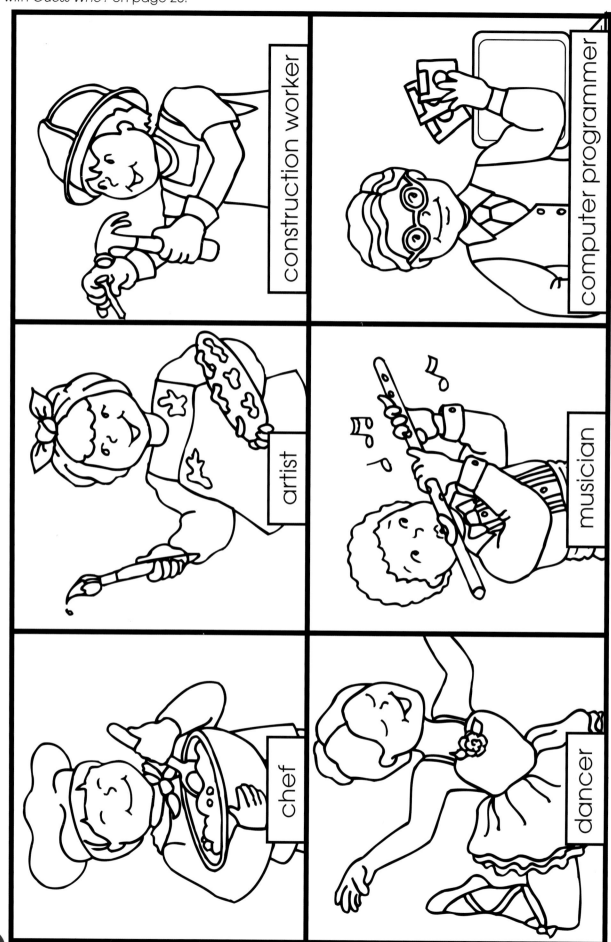

construction worker

computer programmer

artist

musician

chef

dancer

A Job for ME!

Give your little ones lots of opportunities to imagine the career possibilities in their futures. Use the activities in this unit to help youngsters play their way to a better understanding of several different occupations.

by Lucia Kemp Henry

Pam Crane

Planting the Seeds of Thought

When you're just starting out in life, deciding what you want to be when you grow up is just as natural as deciding whether to have a grape, a cherry, or an orange drink. The beauty of it is that a few days later, you're free to change your mind and envision another possible career option. Use prop boxes and literature to stimulate youngsters' thoughts about all the occupations that there are to choose from. For each occupation that you want to feature, decorate and label the outside of a lidded box. Then fill the box with clothing, equipment, and at least one children's book that relates to that career. (See the book list on page 27.) One at a time, introduce the boxes to your students, so that students can discuss contacts they have had with people who do the featured job, talk about how the equipment and clothing are helpful to the worker, and hear the related story. Later place the box where students can use its elements for role-playing.

Being a Grown-Up

Read "When I Grow Up" (right) to your children to stimulate their career-related thoughts. Afterwards, list the following six category headings on a chalkboard and place an item similar to the one listed in parentheses near each heading: "Transportation Jobs" (toy tractor-trailer), "Jobs Selling Things" (grocery and department store bags, slightly stuffed), "Outside Jobs" (toy shovel), "Jobs Making Things" (pieces of wood with nails and scraps of fabric with thread), "Jobs Helping People" (stethoscope or blood-pressure monitor), and "Jobs Helping Animals" (stuffed toy dog). Then ask students to brainstorm all of the careers that they can think of. As each career is mentioned, note it on the board beneath the appropriate category. Then give students opportunities for discussing the pros and cons of the different types of work.

When I Grow Up

Someday soon
When I grow up,
I'll have a job to do.
I'll write a book,
Or be a cook,
Or work inside a zoo.

I might want
To drive a bus
Or teach children to read.
I'll load a train,
Or fly a plane,
Or plant a little seed.

I might want
To fight a fire
Or be a doctor, too.
I'll build a house,
Or sew a blouse,
Or sail the ocean blue.

So many jobs
That I might choose.
I wonder what I'll be.
I'll work and learn,
'Til it's my turn
To find a job for me!

—*by Lucia Kemp Henry*

What Do You Do?

Youngsters will be eager to join in on these verses that highlight the jobs of community helpers. Recite each verse and have youngsters take turns telling about each job and how doing this job benefits others.

What Do You Do?

Teacher, Teacher,
What do you do?
I teach you reading
And writing, too.

Doctor, Doctor,
What do you do?
I help when you're sick
With a cold or a flu.

Counselor, Counselor,
What do you do?
I help you with problems
And I care about you.

Firefighter, Firefighter,
What do you do?
I help fight fires
That might hurt you.

Officer, Officer,
What do you do?
I help you stay safe
In all that you do.

Dentist, Dentist,
What do you do?
I clean your teeth
And keep your gums
    healthy, too.

Children, Children,
What will you do?
When you grow up,
Which job is for you?

—by Lucia Kemp Henry

A Job for Me

These personalized booklets make it easy for each student to imagine himself in a variety of different occupations. In preparation for this activity, reproduce a classroom quantity of the booklet pages on pages 28–33. Ask a few parent volunteers to use X-acto® knives to cut out the dotted circles on the booklet pages and to assemble each child's booklet between construction-paper covers. To finalize the preparations for this activity, ask the volunteers to trace and cut a hole from the front cover of each booklet as shown and glue a child's school photo or self-portrait (or a photocopy of the child's school photo) to the inside back cover of the booklet, so that the child's face is centered in the circular cutouts.

Ask each youngster to write or copy a title and his name on the front cover of his booklet. Then have each student complete the sentence on each page (provide assistance as necessary) and draw pictures or glue on magazine pictures that illustrate his sentence. After writing and gluing (or drawing) on booklet page 28, have each student write his name in the upper left corner as the guest of the day. This done, each youngster will have a booklet that can really spur his imagination about what his future holds.

Paper-Plate Portraits

"This is me. I'm going to be a race car driver when I grow up!" After completing these one-of-a-kind projects, each of your students will be eager to talk about what he plans to do when he grows up. Provide thin paper plates, construction paper, yarn, crayons, glue, and other art supplies, and have each youngster use these supplies to create a self-portrait. Trace each youngster's hands on skin-toned paper and have him cut out the hand-shaped designs. (Provide assistance as necessary.) Have each student glue his hand cutouts to the upper corners of a 12" x 18" sheet of construction paper. Staple the bottom of his paper-plate self-portrait to the construction paper. Then ask the student what career he's considering. On the construction paper, complete the sentence "I can be a..." to reflect the student's response.

If desired, further personalize each student's project by attaching a photograph or drawing of the child properly outfitted for the career he has chosen. (If you're using prop boxes like those mentioned in "Planting the Seeds of Thought," students can wear the dress-up items that the boxes contain for this photo opportunity.)

What Do You Do at Work?

In preparation for this game, decorate a container and fill it with index cards that feature magazine pictures of workers. Have the children stand in a circle, holding hands. Place the card-filled container in the center of the circle and choose one child to stand by the container. As his classmates walk around him humming the tune to "The Farmer in the Dell," have the first student draw a card from the container, decide what the occupation is, and decide how he could act out the job. When his classmates stop singing and walking at the end of the verse, have him act out the pictured job. When a student thinks he knows the occupation being acted out, he sits. The child in the center then chooses a seated student to guess his occupation. When someone guesses correctly, the child in the center describes some of the things a person with this job might do and then tells what he was doing. The youngster who correctly identified the occupation gets the next turn to be in the center and choose a card. The students again walk and hum around the student in the center, and the game continues as before.

Whose Tools Are These?

Cooperation is the key to this sorting activity. Gather lots of job-specific tools, collecting several, if possible, for each job featured in this activity. You may want to use real tools, toy imitations, or a combination of both. For an artist, you might have paints, brushes, paper, and other art supplies. For a coach, you might include a whistle, different types of balls, an empty sports drink bottle, and a clipboard. For a carpenter, provide things such as a tool belt, a hammer, nails, and pieces of wood. Place all the items in a central location in no particular order. Divide the students into small groups and assign each group the task of finding all of the tools specific to one particular job. Allow for lots of discussion as each group works to find the tools for its assigned job. When each group has reached a final decision, ask group members to tell why the tools they chose are needed for the job they were assigned. Since some tools are appropriate for more than one job, be accepting of even the most creative responses.

Career-Related Books

A Carpenter by Douglas Florian (Greenwillow Books)
Airport by Byron Barton (Crowell Jr. Books)
Charlie Parker Played Be-Bop by Chris Raschka (Orchard Books Watts)
Fire! Fire! by Gail Gibbons (Crowell Jr. Books)
The Furry News: How to Make a Newspaper by Loreen Leedy (Holiday House, Inc.)
Going Lobstering by Jerry Pallotta (Charlesbridge Publishing)
Going to the Doctor by Fred Rogers (Putnam)
I Can Be a Farmer by Kathy Henderson (Children's Press)
I Can Be a Forest Ranger by Carol Greene (Children's Press)
I Can Be an Astronaut by June Behrens (Children's Press)
If I Drove a Bus by Miriam Burt Young (Lothrop)
My Dog Is Lost! by Ezra Jack Keats (Crowell Jr. Books)
My Father Is in the Navy by Robin McKinley (Greenwillow Books)
People Working by Douglas Florian (Crowell Jr. Books)
The Post Office Book by Gail Gibbons (Crowell Jr. Books)
The Purple Coat by Amy Hest (Four Winds Press)
Recycle! A Handbook for Kids by Gail Gibbons (Little, Brown, & Co.)
Teachers: A to Z by Jean Johnson (Walker & Co.)
We Keep a Store by Anne Shelby (Orchard Books Watts)
Whose Hat? by Margaret Miller (Greenwillow Books)
Guess Who? by Margaret Miller (Greenwillow Books)
My Apron by Eric Carle (Putnam)

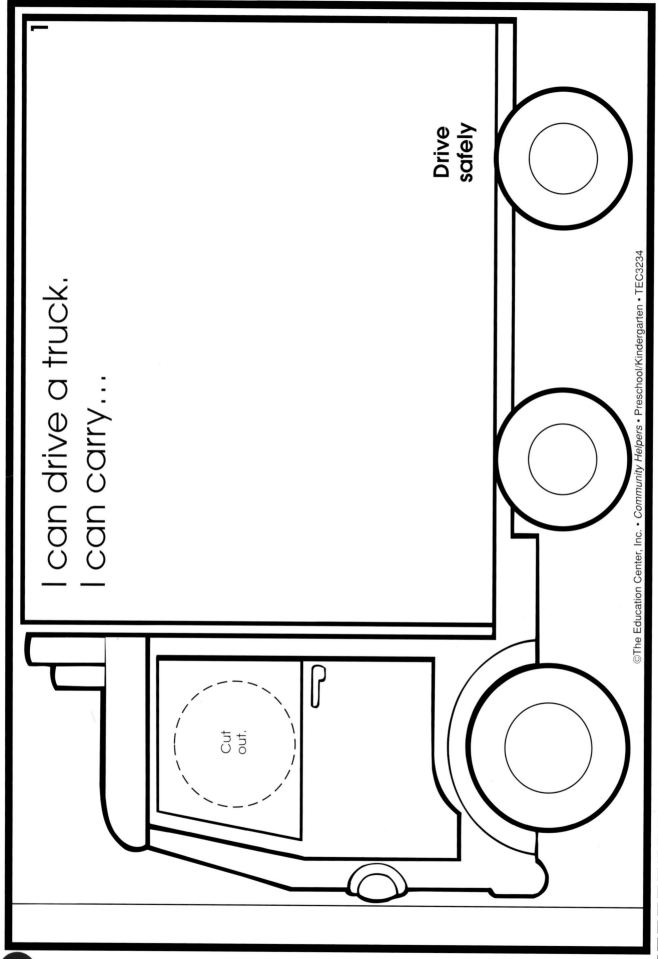

I can drive a truck.
I can carry...

Drive
safely

Cut
out.

28

Note to the teacher: Use with "A Job for Me" on page 26.

2

I can work outside.
I can be a...

Cut out.

©The Education Center, Inc. • *Community Helpers* • Preschool/Kindergarten • TEC3234

Note to the teacher: Use with "A Job for Me" on page 26.

29

3

I can work in a store.
I can sell....

Today's
Special
99¢

Cut
out.

30

4

I can make things.
I can make . . .

Cut out.

©The Education Center, Inc. • *Community Helpers* • Preschool/Kindergarten • TEC3234

Note to the teacher: Use with "A Job for Me" on page 26.

31

I can help people or animals.
I can be a....

Cut out.

Note to the teacher: Use with "A Job for Me" on page 26.

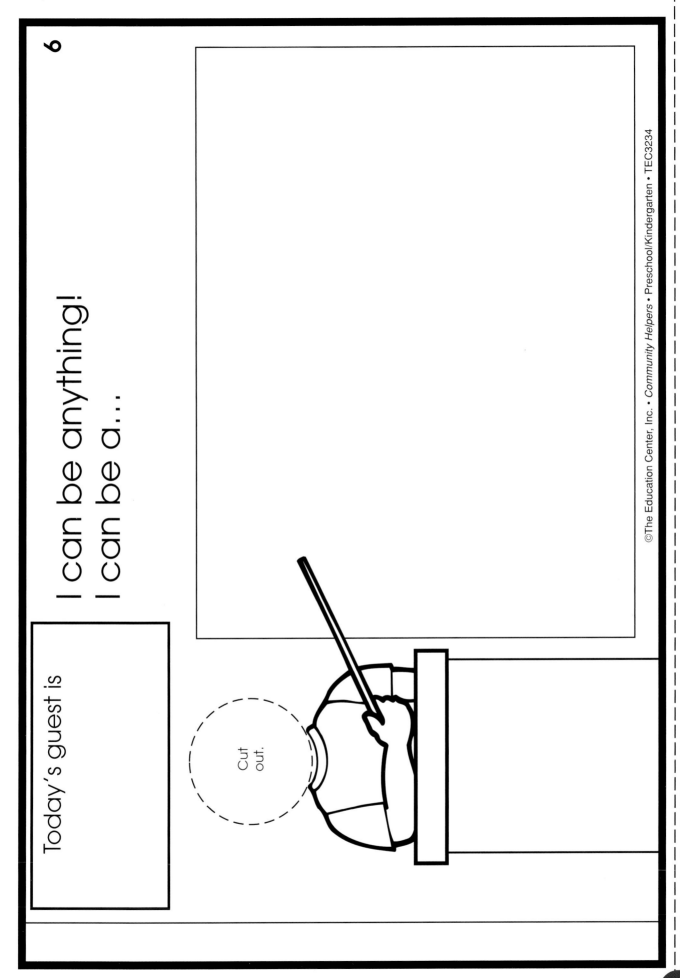

6

I can be anything!
I can be a...

Today's guest is

Cut
out.

Note to the teacher: Use with "A Job for Me" on page 26.

Dressed to Impress

Let imaginations soar with this fun dress-up center. Fill a chest or box with typical and novelty items of clothing. For example, you might include a shirt with buttons, a shirt with snaps, and a jacket with a zipper, as well as gloves, dressy scarves, and various types of hats. As each child visits the center, encourage her to dress to impress. Then, using a Polaroid camera, take a picture of each child. Ask the child to dictate whom she is pretending to be or what she could imagine doing in her new attire. Display the photo along with the dictation in the center. Very impressive!

I am a builder. I will build a house.
Bethany

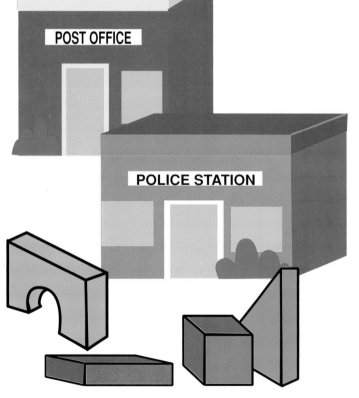

Neighborhood Boxes

What's new around the neighborhood? Buildings for your block area! Collect boxes in a variety of sizes and shapes such as jewelry boxes, shoeboxes, and milk cartons. Have youngsters paint the boxes with tempera paints. Then have them use markers and construction paper to add features such as windows and doors. Help the children label the buildings to denote a purpose for each one—gas station, hospital, post office, school, police station, etc. Then invite your young community planners to go to town in the block center!

Nancy Slotnick—Three- and Four-Year-Olds
The Kids' Space
Braintree, MA

Helper Ideas • • • • •

I'm a Firefighter

(sung to the tune of "I'm a Little Teapot")

I'm a firefighter.   *Point to self.*
Here's my hose.   *Outstretch arm with finger pointed.*
I put out fires
As everyone knows.
When I see a fire   *Hand over brow.*
I douse it out.   *Outstretch arm with finger pointed.*
"Thank you! Thank you!"
People shout!

Linda Rice Ludlow
Bethesda Christian School
Brownsburg, IN

The Doctor's Song

A doctor might sing this song in February. After all, it *is* American Heart Month!

(sung to the tune of "Row, Row, Row Your Boat")

I use a stethoscope
To listen to your heart,
To help you be a healthy child
And heal you when you aren't.

The Mail Carrier's Song

This first-class song makes a perfect addition to a post office unit.

(sung to the tune of "Row, Row, Row Your Boat")

Write, write, write your cards,
And lots of letters, too.
I will bring them to your friends,
And they will write back soon.

Cindy Wunderlich—Preschool
St. Luke's United Methodist Child Development Center
Orlando, FL

35

Classroom Community

Turn your classroom into a mini-neighborhood when you study communities! Hang a sign on your door welcoming visitors to the neighborhood. Then add simple props and costumes to your centers to transform them into different neighborhood locations. For example, turn your housekeeping area into a restaurant with menus for the guests, and notepads and pencils for the waiters. Turn your block area into a fire station with fire hats, hoses (made of wrapping-paper tubes with silver tinsel water), and red and orange tissue-paper fire to attach to block buildings. Make the writing area a post office with a mailbox (made from a blue painted box with a slit cut in the top for letters), stamps, envelopes, paper, and mailbags. Convert your art area into a bakery with play dough, cookie cutters, rolling pins, birthday candles, trays, chefs' hats, and aprons. Welcome, neighbor!

Amy Aloi—Four-Year-Olds
Berkshire Elementary
Forestville, MD

Neighborhood Alphabet

The letters of the alphabet are running amok in your neighborhood! Capture each one in a photo and bring it into the classroom to help your youngsters learn the alphabet. While out and about in your community, simply take pictures of businesses, such as McDonalds, and community buildings, such as the library, that are familiar to your students. Take pictures until you have at least one photo to represent each letter, if possible. Display the photos and corresponding letter cutouts at students' eye level. Or alphabetically label each page of a photo album and place the pictures on the appropriate pages. Before long, your students will be able to identify letters all around them in their neighborhood.

Pat Coleman—Pre-K
Red Bridge Early Childhood Center
Kansas City, MO

Kiely Miller
St. Thomas More School
Kansas City, MO

Medical Center

If you're studying doctors and nurses, why not transform your dramatic play area into a medical center for a few weeks? Decorate the walls with posters donated by a local doctor's office. Provide a white, button-up shirt or scrubs to serve as a doctor's coat or nurse's attire. Then add props such as a toy doctor's kit (with stethoscope, thermometer, reflex hammer, and other tools), wrap-style bandages, and cotton balls. Include a clipboard, pencils, and pads of paper for filling out forms and writing prescriptions. Your young physicians, nurses, and their patients will love it!

Jennifer Barton
Elizabeth Green School
Newington, CT

A
3 F 7
W G K 1
P O M B V
S Q 4 5 7 9
C X Z U L F E
R Y 7 8 5 3 C G

The Optometrist's Office

A visit to the optometrist's office is a great way to boost youngsters' letter and number recognition. Program different sheets of poster board with letters and numbers to resemble eye charts. To create special reading glasses, remove the lenses from several pairs of old eyeglasses or sunglasses. Select one child to don an old white shirt and become the optometrist. Have the optometrist select a "patient." The patient slips on a pair of the special glasses, then "reads" the chart as the optometrist points to a letter or number. The optometrist "checks" each of his patient's responses. If an error is made, he changes the patient's prescription, giving him a different pair of eyeglasses to try. When the chart has been "read" correctly, the patient becomes the optometrist and selects a new patient.

Marilyn Erickson
Lake of the Woods School
Baudette, MN

Look Familiar?

Inspire budding architects by providing photographs of buildings in your community. Take pictures of your school, local fast-food restaurants, a hospital, and other buildings your children may recognize. Laminate the photos; then label the backs of them. Store them in your block center or temporarily mount them on the wall so that they are visible to children seated on the floor and can be removed for closer study. Also include examples of environmental print from the pictured locations. For example, include a bag or coupons from a drug store or paper goods from a fast-food restaurant.

You're the Teacher Now!

What young student doesn't love to pretend to be the grown-up teacher? Entice your little ones into this reading-and-writing center by offering them the chance to do just that! To prepare, make a dry-erase board by laminating a large sheet of poster board. Place the board on an easel in a center along with a supply of dry-erase markers, an eraser (or tissues), and concept books that feature simple topics, such as shapes and the ABCs. Invite children to visit this center, prompting them to role-play students and teachers. Before you know it, this class will be in full session!

Betsy Ruggiano—Gr. K
Victor Mravlag School #21
Elizabeth, NJ

Reproducible Activities...

U.S. MAIL

Oral Instructions

1. Your worksheet looks like a newspaper. This newspaper is called the *Neighborhood News* and has articles about people in the neighborhood. People in your neighborhood can help you. Let's find out who they are and how they help you.

2. Find the picture of the person with the letter. What is his job? *(mail carrier, postal worker)* How can he help you? Color his hat blue.

3. Find the picture of the person with a badge on her shirt. What is her job? *(sheriff, police officer)* How can she help you? Color her hat brown.

4. Find the picture of the person with a big hat. What is his job? *(firefighter)* How can he help you? Color his hat red.

5. Look at the last box. The words in this empty box say "A Good Neighbor." Draw a picture of a neighbor who is helpful to you. Finish coloring the pictures.

Follow-up Activity

Use the real newspaper to extend and enrich this unit. Find articles in your local paper about community and neighborhood helpers, and bring them in to read to your children. Children may even enjoy looking for articles with their parents to bring in and share with the class.

Language Enrichment

The following books will enrich this unit on the neighborhood:

Who Keeps Us Safe? by Caroline Arnold
Who Works Here? by Caroline Arnold
People Working by Douglas Florian
My Dog Is Lost! by Ezra Jack Keats
My Mother the Mail Carrier by Inez Maury
City Workers by Jeanne A. Rowe
Richard Scarry's Postman Pig and His Busy Neighbors by Richard Scarry
I Know a Salesperson by Barbara Williams
If I Drove a Bus by Miriam Burt Young
Dear Garbage Man by Gene Zion

Name_____

Neighborhood News

Vol. 1   No. 1   "All the news in the neighborhood"   25 cents

People in the News

You can meet people in your neighborhood.
They can help you.
Listen and do. Color.

A Letter-Perfect Person

She's on the Beat

He Is Hot Stuff

A Good Neighbor

Oral Instructions

1. Neighborhoods have stores where people can buy things. The stores have ads or advertisements in the newspaper so people know what is on sale. Look at your *Neighborhood News* ad for a Sidewalk Sale, and let's see what's on sale.
2. Find the ad for shoes. What kind of store is it? *(shoe store)* What kind of shoes are these? Color the shoes. Circle your favorite.
3. Find the ad for food. What kind of store is it? *(grocery, market, food)* What foods do you see? Color the pear yellow and the bread brown.
4. Find the ad for T-shirts. What kind of store is it? *(clothing, sports store)* Color a design on the top T-shirt.
5. Find the ad for paint. What kind of store is it? *(hardware, variety, paint, building supply)* Color the paint can, brush, and roller your favorite color.

Follow-up Activity

Provide advertisement sections from several newspapers. Allow the children to look through the papers for ads for items they recognize. Cut out and paste the ads to a large sheet of construction paper. Record dictation about the items the children found on sale. Help them "read" to find out how much the items cost.

Name _____

Neighborhood

You can buy things in your neighborhood.

Listen and do.

 Color.

Sidewalk SALE

Visit your friendly NEIGHBORHOOD stores!

Cool Shoes Store

All shoes on sale!

Neighborhood Hardware

25% Off Paint Sale!

The T-shirt Shop

Buy 2—Get 1 FREE!

Good Neighbor Market

Pears
59¢ a pound

Bread
$1.00

Oral Instructions
for Page 45

1. A neighborhood has special places where you can do many things. The newspaper often tells you what is happening at these special places. Let's read our *Neighborhood News* to find out what's happening.
2. Find the place where you can read. What is this place? What else can you do at the library? Color the books in the picture.
3. Find the place where you can sign up for soccer. What is this place? What else can you do in the park? Color your favorite playground equipment.
4. Find the place where you can get wet. What is this place? What things can you do at the pool? Color the water blue. Color the children.
5. Find the picture of the bus. What kind of bus is it? What can you learn at school? Color the bus yellow.
6. All these pictures tell about what you can do in your neighborhood. Use your red crayon and trace the box around the thing you would like to do the most.

Follow-up Activity

Glean your local neighbors section of your newspaper and cut out articles or ads about activities in the community. Bring these in and read to your children to keep them informed about what is going on that is of interest to them. Allow children to bring in and share articles too.

How to Use Page 46

1. Duplicate one copy of this worksheet for each child.
2. **Before passing out the worksheets,** introduce the story starter on this sheet in a large group, and begin some brainstorming. List responses on a chart pad to form a word bank.
3. After all have had a chance to respond, pass out the worksheets and allow each child to complete the story starter by drawing something that is special in his neighborhood. Children may choose to draw a special place, their house or apartment, or their neighborhood friends.
4. Allow those children who are writing and spelling to write their story completions about their special neighborhood drawings on the manuscript lines provided. Others may dictate.
5. Collect the finished pages and staple into a class book. A copy of the worksheet that has been duplicated on construction paper makes a great cover. Gather the children together and allow each child to read his page aloud.

What's Happening?

Neighborhood PLACES in the *Neighborhood News*

You can do things in your neighborhood.
Listen and do.
✏️ Color.

Let's Play Soccer.

Sign up at the Neighborhood Park.

LIBRARY

Come in and READ!

Come to school.

Open House

STOP

7:00 Tonight

The Neighborhood Pool is cool!

This is my neighborhood.
My neighborhood is special because...

46

Neighborhood Concentration Game

How to Use Page 48

1. Reproduce on construction paper for sturdiness and so pictures will not show through when playing Concentration.
2. Discuss the pictures, identifying the neighborhood helpers and objects. They are: *repairman or carpenter and tools, grocer and food, doctor and health equipment, mailperson and letters, firefighter and truck, policeman and car, librarian and book cart.*
3. Color and cut out the cards.
4. Play the game with two players. (Both their sets of cards may be used simultaneously, if desired.) Turn the cards over in rows so pictures do not show. Mix up pairs. The first player turns over two cards. If the cards match a neighborhood helper and his object, the player keeps the cards. If the cards do not match, they are turned over again and it is the other player's turn. A correct match earns another turn. Play proceeds until all the matches have been made and the cards are picked up. The player with the most cards wins.
5. Send the cards home with the note below in a Ziploc bag for continued learning.

Dear Parent,

Your child has been learning about the neighborhood, and about people and their jobs in the neighborhood. Help your child review what he or she has learned while playing a Concentration game.

The cards in this game show neighborhood helpers (repairman or carpenter, grocer, postal worker, firefighter, librarian, police officer, and doctor) and items they use in their jobs (tools, foods, letters, fire truck, book cart, police car, and medical equipment). Your child should match each neighborhood helper with the things he uses in his job.

To play Concentration, turn all the cards upside down and mix. Arrange them in neat rows. Each player turns over two cards in a turn. If the cards match, the player keeps the cards and goes again. If the cards do not match, the player turns them facedown again. All players try to remember where cards are so when a mate appears, they can turn up a pair on their next turn. Play until all the cards are matched.

For extra fun, allow your child to suggest other neighborhood helpers or careers and their tools, and make additional cards to extend the game. Talk with your child about neighborhood helpers, what they do for the neighborhood, and how they help you and your child.

Have fun concentrating on the neighborhood!

Name

Neighborhood Concentration

Color.

Cut.

Match.

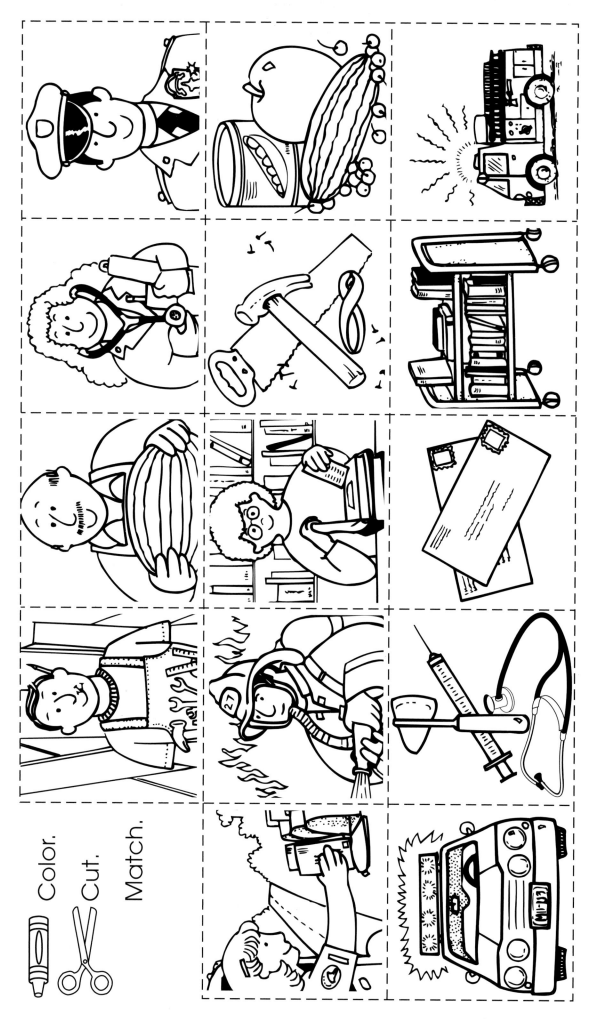